Table Of Contents

INTRODUCTION

Food in bowls was brought by Barack Obama from Hawaii, making this the most democratic gastronomic trend of our century.

The most fashionable food is now served not in porcelain, not on elegant boards, but in deliberately rough bowls. The Wall Street Journal defines bowls as, "the new plates," and this insanity has been triumphantly sweeping the world for three years, conquering even the most advanced institutions - from London to California. And even at the last royal wedding - Prince Harry and Megan Markle (now the Duchess of Sussex) ate a fricassee from a farm chicken with morels and leek, the main hot dish, also served in bowls.

Although in Dickens's time, such utensils were more likely associated with Oliver Twist's orphanage, or at best with the peasant's table, at which was eaten a semi-liquid soup brewed from everything that was found in the cellar. How did the bowl go from beggar to prince?

OBAMA AND HIS HAWAIIAN BOWLS

Until recently in Europe, the symbol of expensive restaurant food was spacious plates, on which cooks laid out small picturesque still lifes. For example: several pieces of fish, two or three bright vegetables and baby greens. Any voluminous mishmash seemed plebeian and reminded of hard military and post-war times when stew was put on a festive table, which was "stretched" with a plentiful side dish, and everyday food was rice and cereals with thick sauces and meat or chicken.

As for the bowls, with their ability to combine different ingredients. Their status began to change with the appearance of fusion fashion in the kitchen, which came from the Hawaiian Islands and gained special popularity under Barack Obama. He is a native of Hawaii, and even in the White House, state receptions often took place in the genre of Luau - Hawaiian gastronomic fiesta, where many dishes are served in bowls. The brand-chef was Alan Wong, the most famous chef from Honolulu, who let loose the idea of fusion.

The first dish in a bowl, which I myself tried, was called moko loco. It looks like this: a hill of rice, on it lies a hamburger, covered with a fried egg, and all this is poured with a dark meat sauce. The sauce is sweet, with light sourness, perfectly Chinese in taste, it's plentiful, and it generously permeates a slightly lime-like rice, which usually happens in sushi, and simple hamburgers without fads, the main advantage of which is freshness. All this together with the liquid yolk of the fried egg is squeezed out of a huge and impossibly deliciously smelling bowl.

POKE, BUT NOT POKÉMON

The main Hawaiian bowl that won over the US and Europe is called pokey (with emphasis on the last syllable), which in translation from pidgin means "small pieces". This dish originated from folk Hawaiian cuisine. It is similar to the Japanese sashimi. The raw fish are cut into cubes, not necessarily even, and seasoned with soy sauce with sesame oil, thinly sliced chives, chopped sweet white onions and hot chili peppers or something else that was at hand - for example, seaweed with nuts or vegetables.

But, as Alan Wong explains, the pike, which was originally just raw fish on rice, then turned into a poke bowl, which was finally formed under the influence of the island's Japanese cuisine, from which came soy sauce, wasabi and sesame oil. Unlike ceviche, poke bowls are more often cooked from fatty raw fish instead of white fish- primarily raw tuna, salmon, trout, but also from octopus or fish in teriyaki sauce. There are also many vegan variants: including tofu, vegetables and fruit.

The growing popularity of this appetizer is explained by the fact that people increasingly like light and healthy dishes from raw or quickly cooked fish and vegetables, without butter or fatty sauces. In addition, poke-bowl is a comfortable dish, where everything is served in one bowl: rice or other grains, beans, greens and proteins.

These bowls with food in the Oriental and Asian style even have a special name - a bowl of the Buddha. What does the Enlightened One have to do with it? After all, the Buddha himself was indifferent to eating. Nevertheless, he, according to legend, ate from a bowl, as is now accepted among Buddhist monks in traditional communities. In their bowls, the gifts of benefactors are the most prominent, therefore such food is called "spiritually realized". For novices, it is often vegetarian: rice, kinoa, farro, tofu, lentils, chickpeas, noodles and vegetables - cooked on the grill, steamed or raw, plus some spicy sauce. Although vegetarianism is not particularly related to Buddhism, and in many communities, they eat everything that they are given by nature. According to one account, it is believed that the Enlightened One himself died having eaten stale meat of boar with rice.

A PLATE FROM THE PEOPLE

So, bowls today can contain breakfasts, and snacks, and lunches, and dinners. But why are they so important? Many people say that everything is tastier in a bowl.

After all, the meal is not only a physiological, but also an aesthetic and psychological process. Scooping up food from a bowl, where it is laid out in thoughtful layers, in each spoonful you grab a complex of textures, flavors and aromas.

And yes, well-made bowls are aesthetic. Moreover, the bowl is a whole revolution in the supply of many beautiful to taste, but ugly dishes. Take, for example, our Beef Stroganoff - deliciously crazy, but on the plate it looks something brown and unsympathetic. The bowl made it possible to hide the saturated meat stews or the equally shapeless fish curry, and make a picturesque dish of bright vegetables, herbs and chips. Even ordinary porridges served in cute bowls and decorated with berries, seeds and mint leaves look very appetizing. This is convenient for cooks and for food-photo lovers; it looks spectacular on Instagram.

When the chef Mark Flanagan was asked why he decided to serve from bowls, the chief replied: "The young people did not want prudish boredom, they set me the task of making dishes that did not interfere with communication." I do not need to eat from a bowl with a knife and a fork - you can stand and talk. " If earlier, the rich and famous wanted to emphasize their elitism, now another trend is emerging. Even the old European aristocracy wants to at least look democratic.

In addition, there is something homemade in bowls, in big megacities comfortable food is again in demand. I myself noticed: when I have a bowl of food in my hand, the mood improves and the world around me looks more friendly.

POKE-BOWL: RECIPE

Preparing this delicious dish at home is not difficult. It is important to buy good quality products and understand how the bowl is "built" and what parts it consists of.

- Base - simple rice or coconut, noodles, legumes, boiled or sprouted cereals, fake "rice" from cauliflower or broccoli.

- The main ingredient is raw, salted or cooked fish, shrimp, octopus, fried or pickled tofu, pumpkin cubes, beets and so on.

- Additional ingredients - pieces of raw or cooked vegetables, seaweed - fried or a salad of them.

- Marinade sauce - aioli-wasabi, teriyaki, miso with ginger, ponzu, garlic-sesame, avocado with soy sauce, pesto, chimichurri.

- Topping - crispy vegetable or grain chips, sprouted greens, fermented or pickled vegetables (including onions), salsa (with mango and other fruits), nuts, fried sesame seeds, dried seaweed.

Now you know everything to cook the best poke on your own! I've broken down the recipes I'm suggesting you to cook into four parts. We'll start off with the easiest recipes and then try to cook traditional Hawaiian and then full meal. I also decided to offer a section with a menu for vegans and those on paleo diets - the Healthy section.

QUICK

STUDENT POKE

A low-cost, low-effort dish perfect for anybody on a budget, but still looking for something bursting with flavour.

Ingredients:

- *A dash of soy sauce*
- *1 teaspoon of sesame oil*
- *2 tablespoons of orange juice*
- *5cm piece of ginger, grated*
- *2 cans of tuna*
- *10g of cilantro*
- *1 scallion, finely chopped*
- *1 cup of white rice, boiled as instructed on packet*
- *1 tomato, chopped into cubes*
- *A pinch of sesame seeds*

Instructions:

- To make the dressing: place the soy sauce, sesame oil, orange juice and ginger in a jar. Shut tightly and shake until the mixture has combined.
- Into a bowl, place the tuna, the scallion and the cilantro. Then add rice and dressing. Mix well.
- Add the tomato and sesame seeds on top and serve.

CHICKEN AND GINGER

Time to Make: 20 min

Calories: 500 Kcal

Serves: 2

A blend of Mediterranean and Japanese flavours, this ginger chicken bowl is guaranteed to provide you with all the nutrients and protein you need to keep you going thorough out the day.

Ingredients:

- *3 cups of brown rice, boiled as instructed on packet*
- *2 cups of diced chicken breast*
- *1/4 cup of green onions, chopped*
- *1 tablespoon of minced garlic, minced*
- *1 tablespoon of soy sauce*
- *1 ½ tablespoon of canola oil*
- *1 1/2 teaspoon of Organic Grated Ginger*

Instructions:

- Mix tamari, garlic, ginger and ½ tablespoon of canola oil with chicken; let sit for 5 minutes.
- Add remaining oil to a pan over a medium heat and cook chicken until firm and brown.
- Place rice in a serving bowl.
- Place chicken top rice and add green onions on top.

SALMON AND MIXED FRUIT POKE

Time to Make: 12min

Calories: 711Kcal

Serves: 2

A perfectly light and quick to make dish, that goes down a treat on a hot Summers day when you just want to be relaxing by the pool or getting on down to the beach.

Ingredients:

- *1 cup of brown rice, boiled as shown on packet*
- *300g of raw wild salmon, sliced into small pieces*
- *1 cup of kale, cress and spinach, chopped into small pieces*
- *1 nectarine, chopped into pieces*
- *½ apple, cut into bite sized chunks*
- *1/2 cup avocado, diced*
- *2 tablespoons of canola oil*
- *A pinch of black sesame seeds*
- *1 tablespoon of raw coconut aminos*
- *½ tablespoon of garlic, minced*
- *1/2 tablespoon of cayenne pepper*

Instructions:

- Place rice in a serving bowl.
- Add the cup of kale, cress and spinach.
- Mix all remaining ingredients into a separate mixing bowl and mix well.
- Place mix on rice and greens. Serve immediately.

PINEAPPLE AND AVOCADO POKE

Time to Make: 10 min
Calories: 270 Kcal
Serves: 2

Mixing the most popular fruit of both Hawaii and California, this Poke bowl is a blend of flavours that will delight your taste buds.

Ingredients:

- *200g of pineapple, diced into 1-inch chunks*
- *1 avocado, cut and diced into small pieces*
- *1 red pepper, cut into very small pieces*
- *A dash of soy sauce*
- *1 cup of brown rice, boiled as indicated on the package*

Instructions:

- Mix the pineapple, avocado, and red pepper into a bowl and add soy sauce.
- Place the rice in a serving bowl and add the mix on top.
- Toss well and serve immediately.

TRADITIONAL

HOMEMADE HEALTHY AHI TUNA POKE BOWLS

Time to Make: 30 mins

Calories: 391 Kcal

Serves: 4

A delicious, easy to make Japan-inspired dish; filled with brown rice, salad and vegetables. Easily fits into any diet plan and is guaranteed to leave you feeling satisfied whilst keeping off the pounds.

Ingredients:

- *0.45kg of sushi-grade ahi tuna, cut into bite-size chunks.*
- *¼ cup of soy sauce*
- *1 ½ Teaspoons of sesame oil*
- *¾ teaspoon of crushed red pepper flakes*
- *1/3 cup of green onions*
- *½ teaspoon of sesame seeds*
- *2 cups of brown rice*
- *2 cups of salad greens (spinach, cucumber, ginger and dried seaweed are good fits)*

Instructions:

- Combine the ahi tuna, soy sauce, rice vinegar, sesame oil, crushed red pepper flakes. Green onions and sesame seeds.
- Add the cooked rice and salad to the bowl.
- Toss to recombine and serve immediately.

MARLIN POKE

Time to Make: 30mins

Calories: 400 Kcal

Serves: 4

Another classic, marlin poke is a traditional Hawaiian dish that really exemplifies everything about the islands culinary culture.

Ingredients:

- *300g of marlin, cut into large dice*
- *¼ cup minced white onion*
- *¼ cup minced scallions*
- *3 tablespoons reddish-brown seaweed, like limu kohu or ogo (see note)*
- *1 tablespoon ground kukui nuts (also known as candlenuts; see note)*
- *2 teaspoons sesame oil*
- *½ teaspoon coarse sea salt*

Instructions:

- In a large bowl, combine the fish, onion, scallions, seaweed and ground kukui nuts and toss gently with a wooden spoon to mix.
- Drizzle with sesame oil and sprinkle with salt. Toss again and serve.

VEGAN HAWAIIAN POKE

Time to Make: 25min

Calories: 420 Kcal

Serves: 4

Whilst the vegan Hawaiian pizza causes much controversy, this delicious dish is guaranteed to keep everyone happy!

Ingredients:

- *1/2 red bell pepper, diced*
- *2 medium-sized carrots, shredded*
- *1/2 cucumber, sliced*
- *1 medium-sized red onion, sliced*
- *2 cups edamame, cooked as shown on packet*
- *4 cups of cooked mixed rice (black and brown), cooked as shown on packet*
- *4 slices of pineapple ring*
- *2 tablespoons olive oil*
- *8 ounces tempeh, thinly sliced and cut diagonally in a triangle shape*
- *1 teaspoon of sesame seeds*
- *1/4 nori sheet, cut into thin stripes*
- *3 tablespoons of teriyaki sauce*

Instructions:

- Divide the rice mixture in four serving bowls. Place the vegetables over the rice and sort by type.
- Heat up a griddle over medium high heat and add the pineapple rings. When the bottoms start to have grill marks, flip over carefully and grill the other side. When both sides of the pineapple slices have grill marks, remove from the griddle. Let them cool slightly before slicing them in half. Place the pineapple on the rice beside the veggies.
- Give the griddle a quick rinse and dry it with a towel. Heat the griddle with medium high heat. When the griddle is hot, add 2

tablespoons of olive oil and the tempeh triangles. Fry both sides until they have brown griddle marks and are cooked through.

- Drizzle the remaining teriyaki sauce over the bowls and garnish with sesame seeds and nori strips. Serve immediately.

ONO POKE

Time to Make: 30 min

Calories: 249 Kcal

Serves: 4

An amazingly simple recipe that still manages to impress even the most die-hard food snobs.

Ingredients:

- *150g ono, cubed*
- *1/2 teaspoon salt*
- *2 tablespoons olive oil*
- *2 limes, juiced*
- *2 Hawaiian chile pepper, minced*
- *1 tablespoon soy sauce*
- *1 teaspoon sesame oil*
- *1 tablespoon green onion, sliced finely*
- *1/2 cup chopped ogo*

Instructions:

- In a mixing bowl, mix ono with salt and olive oil then add the remaining ingredients. Serve cold.

SPICY PONZU POKE

Time to Make: 40min

Calories: 600 Kcal

Serves: 4

A Japanese seafood classic, ponzu sauce pairs well with the Hawaiian culinary seafood tradition.

Ingredients:

- *2 cups sushi rice, cooked as shown on packet*
- *400ml water*
- *80ml sushi rice seasoning*
- *600g sashimi-grade salmon, skinned & pin-boned*
- *50ml soy sauce*
- *25ml mirin*
- *50ml rice vinegar*
- *20ml lemon juice*
- *2 tsp bonito flakes*
- *2 tbsp sesame oil*
- *1 tbsp Sriracha sauce*
- *1 tbsp mirin*
- *½ daikon radish, finely grated*
- *½ Spanish onion, finely grated*
- *1 clove garlic, finely grated*
- *½ daikon radish, julienned*
- *2 red capsicums, julienned*
- *1 bunch red radish, finely sliced*
- *2 spring onions, finely sliced*
- *½ cucumber, sliced into ribbons*
- *1 nori sheet, sliced into ribbons*
- *1 punnet beach bananas*
- *toasted sesame seeds*
- *fried shallots*
- *Korean chilli powder*

Instructions:

- For the ponzu sauce – mix the soy, mirin, rice vinegar, lemon juice and bonito flakes together in a saucepan. Bring to the boil, then remove from the heat and leave for 1 hour. In a mixing bowl, combine thoroughly with the remaining ingredients.
- To serve – dice the salmon and marinate in the ponzu sauce for 2 minutes. Scoop some rice into each bowl, then top with salmon and thinly sliced vegetables. Finish with nori, fried shallots, sesame seeds and Korean chilli powder.

CURRIED CALAMARI POKE

Time to Make: 45min

Calories: 487 Kcal

Serves: 4

A light and flavourful dish, Grapefruit and lime juice work here as the citrusy base, and mango adds a tropical twist.

Ingredients:

- 2 cups water, plus more for the ice water bath
- 2 Cups of white rice, boiled as shown on packet
- 12 ounces cleaned calamari, bodies cut into 1/2-inch rings and tentacles left whole
- 1/2 cup freshly squeezed grapefruit juice (from about 1 grapefruit)
- 1/2 teaspoon finely grated lime zest
- 1/2 cup freshly squeezed lime juice (from about 5 limes), plus more as needed
- 1/2 small red onion, finely chopped
- 2 tablespoons minced shallot (from about 1/2 medium shallot)
- 1 medium garlic clove, minced
- 1/2 serrano chili, stemmed, seeded, and minced
- 1/4 teaspoon curry powder
- 1 medium mango, peeled and cut into medium dice
- 1/4 cup thinly sliced red radishes (from about 2 medium radishes)
- Kosher salt
- Freshly ground black pepper
- 3 medium avocado

Instructions:

- Prepare an ice water bath by filling a large bowl halfway with ice and water; set aside.
- Bring the measured water to a boil over high heat in a medium saucepan. Add the calamari, stir, and cook until just opaque, about 1 minute. Remove with a slotted spoon to the ice water bath and let cool, about 4 to 5 minutes. Remove the calamari from the

ice water bath and spread out on a clean kitchen towel or paper towels to dry.

- Place the grapefruit juice, lime zest, lime juice, onion, shallot, garlic, serrano, and curry powder in a large bowl and stir to combine. Add the dry calamari, rice, mango, and radishes, season with salt and pepper, and stir to combine. Cover and refrigerate for at least 2 hours and up to 6 hours. Taste and season with additional salt, pepper, and lime juice as needed.
- Peel the avocados, cut them in half, and remove the pits. To serve, mound about a quarter of the ceviche onto each avocado half.

FRIED SPINACH AND TOMATO

Time to Make: 45min

Calories: 780 Kcal

Serves: 6

An Indian- inspired dish, this deliciously creamy Poke bowl is certainly unusual, but still delicious and filling.

Ingredients:

- *1 cup of yoghurt sauce*
- *1 cup gram flour*
- *1 cup of tamarind sauce*
- *¼ teaspoon of deggi mirch*
- *1/4 teaspoon ground tummeric*
- *1 cup water*
- *1 teaspoon salt*
- *8 ounces fresh baby spinach leaves*
- *6 cups canola oil, for deep-frying*
- *1/2 teaspoon Toasted Cumin Powder*
- *1/2 teaspoon black salt*
- *1/2 cup finely chopped red onion*
- *2 medium tomatoes, center pulp and seeds removed, finely chopped (1/2 cup)*
- *1/4 cup chopped fresh cilantro*
- *2 cups of white rice, boiled as shown on packet*

Instructions:

- In a NutriBullet or small blender, blend the gram flour, deggi mirch, turmeric, salt, and water until smooth. Pour into a small bowl.
- Have ready two large bowls, a colander set over a plate or bowl, and two baking sheets lined with paper towels. Divide the spinach into four 2-ounce piles.
- Pour the oil into a wok or kadai and heat to 400°F

- In a large bowl, coat all the leaves in one pile of spinach with ¼ cup (a 2-ounce ladle) of batter. You can use a rubber spatula to fold the batter over the leaves, but your hand is a more efficient tool. (Have a towel handy to wipe it on as you work).
- Drop the leaves in the oil, covering the entire surface area rather than just clumping everything in the center of the wok. (The leaves will spatter and emit steam as the water in them comes in contact with the oil and evaporates.) Working quickly, use a spider strainer or a skimmer to circulate the leaves and keep them from sticking to each other as best you can. Fry until the leaves look crisp and the batter lightly browned, 60 to 80 seconds. Using the spider strainer, transfer the spinach to the colander, tilting it to let excess frying oil drain. Then transfer the spinach to the paper towels.
- Repeat with the remaining three batches of spinach and batter, allowing the oil to return to 400°F each time and using the spider strainer or a skimmer to remove as many particles of fried batter from the oil as you can. Discard any leftover batter.
- Place all the fried spinach in the second large bowl. Sprinkle the cumin powder, deggi mirch, and black salt over it and toss the leaves gently to distribute the spices evenly.
- To serve, pile the spinach and rice on six serving plates and drizzle with yogurt sauce and tamarind sauce. Garnish with the red onion, tomatoes, and cilantro. Serve immediately so the leaves don't get soggy.

BRUSSEL SPROUTS WITH KIMCHI AND BACON POKE

Time to Make: 45min

Calories: 1,120 Kcal

Serves: 4

A curious dish, this Poke has a very central European character that certainly accentuates the savoury flavours it presents.

Ingredients:

- *1 cup Napa Cabbage Kimchi*
- *4 ounces thick-cut smoked bacon, cut crosswise into 1/4-inch pieces*
- *500g Brussels sprouts, bottoms trimmed and cut in half through the core*
- *Kosher salt*
- *Freshly ground black pepper*
- *2 tablespoons unsalted butter (1/4 stick), cut into 4 pieces*
- *1 cup peeled, grated carrots (about 2 to 3 medium), grated on the large holes of a box grater*

Instructions:

- Heat the oven to 400°F and arrange a rack in the middle.
- Place the kimchi in the bowl of a food processor fitted with a blade attachment and process until puréed (the mixture will not be smooth), stopping often and scraping down the sides of the bowl with a rubber spatula, about 3 to 4 minutes. Transfer to a small saucepan; set aside.
- Place the bacon in a large oven-safe frying pan over medium heat and cook, stirring occasionally, until crisp, about 9 to 10 minutes. Transfer with a slotted spoon to a paper-towel-lined plate; set aside.
- Remove the pan from heat. Remove and discard all but 1 tablespoon of bacon fat from the pan. Arrange the Brussels sprouts in the pan, cut side down and in a single layer, and season with salt and pepper. Roast in the oven until the cut sides are golden brown, about 8 to 10 minutes. Stir the Brussels sprouts and continue roasting until knife tender, about 10 to 15 minutes more.

- Meanwhile, place the saucepan of puréed kimchi over low heat until simmering. Keep warm.
- When the Brussels sprouts are ready, remove from the oven, add the butter and reserved bacon, and stir to combine. Taste and season with salt and pepper as needed (keep in mind that the puréed kimchi may be salty).
- To serve, divide the puréed kimchi among 4 shallow bowls. Using the back of a spoon, spread the purée out so that it covers the bottom of the bowls. Divide the Brussels sprouts and bacon among the bowls, followed by a mound of the grated carrots. Serve immediately.

FULL MEAL

PINEAPPLE AND CHORIZO POKE

Time to Make: 40min

Calories: 1,200 Kcal

Serves: 2

Another blend of Mediterranean and Hawaiian flavours, classic Spanish chorizo contrasts against the sweetness of pineapple to create a stunningly good dish.

Ingredients:

- *2 cups white rice, boiled as instructed on packet*
- *1 tablespoon olive oil*
- *1/2 sweet onion, diced*
- *2 garlic cloves, minced*
- *100g chorizo, chopped and removed from the casing (if needed)*
- *1/2 teaspoon salt*
- *1/2 teaspoon pepper*
- *1/2 teaspoon smoked paprika*
- *1 tablespoon unsalted butter*
- *1 1/2 cups pineapple, chopped into 1-inch chunks*
- *6 to 8 sweet mini bell peppers, sliced*
- *4 green onions, thinly sliced*

Instructions:

- Heat a pan to a medium heat and add the olive oil, along with the chorizo, the onion and the garlic. Stir for 5 min. Add to a bowl.
- Keep the pan on medium and add butter. Add pineapple and stir, cooking until slightly caramelized. Stir in the sliced peppers and cook for 5 more minutes, stirring often.
- Add the chorizo and rice back to the pan. Stir in the green onion. Reduce the heat to low. Toss everything together and stir until it all warms. Scoop servings into bowl. Serve with lime wedges.

HOT AND SOUR SHRIMP

Time to Make: 10min

Calories: 540 Kcal

Serves: 2

Made with delicious bamboo rice, this vitamin fuelled bowl is characteristically South-East Asian in its flavour.

Ingredients:

- *3 cups bamboo rice, boiled as instructed on packet*
- *1 1/2 cups cooked shrimp*
- *1 sweet onion, chopped finely*
- *2 tablespoons of lime juice*
- *2 tablespoons of rice vinegar*
- *1 tablespoon of canola oil*
- *1/2 tablespoon of wasabi*
- *1 tablespoon soy sauce*

Instructions:

- In a mixing bowl, toss shrimp and onions with all ingredients except rice.
- Place rice at base of serving bowl, add shrimp mix on top.
- Serve immediately.

PORK-NOODLE POKE

Time to Make: 35 min
Calories: 720 Kcal
Serves: 2

A very flavourful dish where the noodles and vegetables really allow for the silky savoury taste of pork to shine through.

Ingredients:

- *1/4 cup soy sauce*
- *3 tablespoon of hoisin sauce*
- *1 lime, juiced*
- *1 tablespoon sriracha*
- *1/2 pack brown rice noodles (approx. 8 oz), boiled as indicated on packet*
- *100g of pork loin, chopped into cubes*
- *2 tablespoons of olive oil*
- *1 cup of edamame beans*
- *1 radish, thinly sliced*
- *1 large carrot, shredded*
- *1/4 cucumber, sliced*
- *1/4 cup pickled red cabbage*
- *Rainbow toasted sesame seeds*

Instructions:

- To make the sauce: mix the soy sauce, hosin sauce, lime juice and sriracha into a bowl.
- Heat olive oil in a pan on medium heat, add the pork, cook until brown.
- Turn off the heat and add half the amount of sauce, Coating the pork.
- Place rice noodles on the base of the bowl, and top with pork, edamame, radish, carrot, cucumber, pickled red cabbage and toasted sesame.
- Use remaining sauce as needed to top your bowl and serve within an hour.

TROUT POKE BOWL

Time to Make: 40min
Calories: 568 Kcal
Serves: 2

An unmistakeably sea-food inspired dish, this bowl departs from the usual tuna Poke and brings something with a bit more kick to the dinner table.

Ingredients:

- *20g of dried wakame seaweed*
- *2 tablespoons of toasted sesame seeds*
- *1 tablespoons of rice wine vinegar*
- *2 tablespoons of freshly grated ginger*
- *2 tablespoons of soy sauce*
- *2 teaspoons of sesame oil*
- *1 radish, finely sliced*
- *1/2 carrot, grated, julienned or spiralized*
- *1 tablespoon of rice wine vinegar*
- *1/2 teaspoon of salt*
- *1 teaspoon of lemon juice*
- *1/2 cup podded edamame beans*
- *1 spring onion, finely sliced*
- *1/3 cup cucumber, chopped in 1 cm dice*
- *1 cup brown rice, cooked as instructed by packet*
- *200g ocean trout (sashimi grade) cut into a 1 cm dice*
- *1 teaspoon of sriracha*

Instructions:

- Place seaweed in a bowl and cover in cold water. Leave for 5 minutes and dry. Squeeze out any water. Add finely chopped spring onion. Mix rice wine vinegar, tamari, maple syrup, sesame oil, ginger and sesame seeds. Pour over spring onion and seaweed. Set aside.

- Place carrot and radish in separate small bowls, season and drizzle vinegar over them. Set aside.
- Mix cucumber, lemon juice and ginger
- Mix the trout with soy sauce, sesame seeds and sesame oil.
- Add the rice to a bowl and place everything on top. Mix well and serve immediately.

MISO POKE

Time to Make: 25min
Calories: 1,200 Kcal
Serves: 2

Miso has always had a place in traditional Japanese cuisine, so it only feels natural when this bowl combines it with classic Hawaiian Poke Bowls.

Ingredients:

- *1 cup of white rice, boiled as instructed on packet*
- *1 medium sweet potato, boiled in water until soft then chopped into 1-inch cubes*
- *2 cups Okinawan Purple Sweet Potato*
- *2 tablespoons of Jalapenos (Chopped)*
- *1/2 teaspoons of Ume Plum Vinegar*
- *1 teaspoon of Kyoto White Miso*
- *1 teaspoon of Lime Juice*
- *1 teaspoon of Coconut Sugar*
- *1 teaspoon of olive oil*

Instructions:

- In a mixing bowl, mix vinegar, miso paste, lime juice, oil and sugar.
- Add sweet potatoes and jalapeno and mix.
- Place rice in a serving bowl and top with sweet potato poke mix and sunomono.

CHILE STEAK AND MACADAMIA

Time to Make: 30min
Calories: 1,355 Kcal
Serves: 2

A heavy, filling dish that departs from the usually light poke bowls to bring a hearty meal to the dinner table.

Ingredients:

- *2 cups of steak, chopped into 1-inch pieces*
- *2 cups of white rice*
- *1 cup Organic Microgreens*
- *1/4 cup of Shallots*
- *1/4 cup of macadamia nuts, raw*
- *3 tablespoons of Minced Garlic*
- *2 tablespoons of Cayenne Pepper chili*
- *1 tablespoons of Tamari Sauce*
- *1/2 tablespoons of Oil, canola*

Instructions:

- Preheat oven to 200 degrees C.
- Mix tamari sauce and oil with half of chili, garlic, and shallot and pour over steak
- Marinate steak for five minutes, then roast in oven on a baking sheet (15 minutes for medium)
- Stir a dash of orange blossom water into jasmine rice and place in a bowl
- Once removed from oven, let steak rest then cut into cubes
- Mix steak and any juices from cutting with macadamias, micro greens and remaining chili, garlic and shallot, and pile atop rice.

CHICKEN POKE BOWL

Time to Make: 30min

Calories: 1,012 Kcal

Serves: 2

Honeyed chicken, char-grilled with soy sauce is a perfect topping for poke bowls and this recipe will not disappoint.

Ingredients:

- *2 cups of white rice, boiled as instructed on packet*
- *1/2 cup of honey*
- *1/4 cup of soy sauce*
- *1/4 cup of sushi seasoning*
- *1/4 cup of fresh lime juice*
- *600g chicken breast fillets, halved horizontally*
- *300g corn cobbs*
- *1 green onion*
- *3 cups of finely shredded green cabbage*
- *1 mango, peeled, diced*
- *Nori sheets, to serve*
- *1 cup of cashews*
- *1 tablespoon of sesame seeds*

Instructions:

- Preheat oven to 160°C. Cook sushi rice following packet Instructions:. Set aside.
- Meanwhile, to make honey sesame cashews; line an oven tray with baking paper. Toss all ingredients on tray. Bake for 15 minutes stirring halfway through until golden and sticky. Remove, set aside to cool.
- In a medium bowl combine honey, soy, sushi seasoning and lime juice. Marinate chicken in 1/4 cup honey soy mixture for 5 minutes. Toss remaining marinade through cooked sushi rice.
- Heat a chargrill on high. Cook corn and onion for 5 minutes, turning, until charred and tender. Cut onions into batons. Grill

chicken for 5 minutes each side or until cooked through. Slice into large pieces.

- Serve rice topped with cabbage, chargrilled vegetables, chicken and mango. Top with honey sesame cashews. Accompany with nori sheets if liked.

TUNA WASABI POKE

Time to Make: 25min
Calories: 968 Kcal
Serves: 2

This hot and spicy dish is not for the faint of pallet, but for those willing to brave the wasabi, it is definitely worth tasting.

Ingredients:

- ¼ cup of soy sauce
- 2 tablespoons of sesame oil
- 2 tablespoons of rice wine vinegar
- 1 tablespoons of wasabi paste
- 500 g sashimi-grade tuna, cut into 1 cm dice
- 270 g ramen noodles, boiled as instructed on packet
- 1½ cups of frozen shelled edamame (soybeans)
- 2 avocados
- Black sesame seeds, crushed wasabi peas, to serve

Instructions:

- In a medium bowl, combine soy, sesame, vinegar and wasabi. Mix with through tuna. Cover in cling film and place in fridge for 30 mins.
- Serve noodles with tuna and avocado. Drizzle with any extra tuna marinade. Accompany with black sesame seeds and crushed wasabi peas to serve, if liked.
- For extra spice, add small red chills, sliced.

CRAB-LEG POKE

Time to Make: 30min

Calories: 1,120 Kcal

Serves: 4

Whilst not for everyone, crustaceans like crab are a delicious addition to rice based dishes like poke, and their light, yet filling meat is guaranteed to satisfy everyone.

Ingredients:

- 1 ½ cup of white rice, cooked as instructed on packet
- 400g of crab leg
- ½ a cup of finely sliced scallions
- ¼ cup of cucumber, peeled
- ½ cup of avocado, diced
- A pinch of sea salt
- 2 tablespoons of canola oil
- 1 teaspoon of toasted sesame seeds
- Siracha mayonnaise
- 1 Tablespoon of nori, shredded finely

Instructions:

- Crack open the crab legs with a hammer or a crab shell breaker (a nutcracker will do) and remove the meat.
- Heat a pan to high heat, place the canola oil on the pan and add the crab leg. Cook for 30-40 seconds.
- Mix the remaining ingredients except for rice in a bowl.
- Dice the crab leg into 1-inch cubes and add to the bowl.
- Add rice to base of a bowl and place mix on top. Serve cool.

RED PEPPER AND SHRIMP POKE

Time to Make: 30 min

Calories: 1,200Kcal

Serves: 4

Inspired by creamy Italian fettucine, this spicy meal is deliciously garlicy and is influenced by Italian roots.

Ingredients:

- *300g of raw, peeled shrimp*
- *8 ounces of white rice, boiled as instructed on packet*
- *200g of roasted red pepper*
- *Juice of 1 lemon*
- *1 teaspoon of chili powder*
- *1 teaspoon of salt*
- *1 tablespoon of olive oil*

Instructions:

- Heat shrimp over a pan on medium heat with olive oil, add salt on top. Sauté for 3 minutes until cooked through. Add red pepper for 30 seconds then remove from heat.
- Place rice at base of serving bowl and add mix of shrimp and pepper. Place lemon juice over the top and sprinkle chili powder. Serve immediately.

JERK SALMON WITH MANGO SAUCE

Time to Make: 30 min

Calories: 1,177 Kcal

Serves: 4

A Caribbean-inspired dish that is full of flavour and very healthy, guaranteed to make you feel good any day of the week.

Ingredients:

- *200g of salmon steak*
- *1 teaspoon oil*
- *1 1/2 teaspoon cumin*
- *1/2 teaspoon curry*
- *1/2 teaspoon chili powder*
- *1/2 teaspoon allspice*
- *1/4 teaspoon cayenne pepper*
- *1/4 teaspoon cinnamon*
- *pinch of sea salt*
- *2 cups of white rice, boiled as instructed on the packet*
- *1 can of black beans, rinsed and drained*
- *2 mangos, peeled and diced*
- *1/2 large red onion, diced*
- *1 bunch fresh cilantro, chopped*
- *1 tablespoon of lime juice*

Ingredients:

- Stir the spices together. Rub over salmon. Sprinkle with sea salt.
- Heat the oil in a pan over medium high heat. Add salmon and cook for 3-5 minutes. Add more oil as necessary to prevent from sticking. Flip the salmon and cook another 3-5 minutes. The salmon will start to get a brown crust on the outside from the spices.
- When salmon is mostly cooked, break up into smallish pieces and leave on heat until completely cooked through (not translucent).

Once the pieces are cooked, remove from heat – salmon dries out quickly if you overcook it.

- Combine mangos, red onion, cilantro, lime juice, and avocado in a small bowl and stir until combined. Season with sea salt.
- Stir together rice and beans and season with several pinches of salt, adding a tablespoon water if necessary.
- Divide between bowls, layering the rice and beans, salmon, and salsa into each bowl.

HOISIN DUCK POKE

Time to Make: 45 min

Calories: 1, 368 Kcal

Serves: 4

A Chinese classic, this bowl is reminiscent of the far orient and is sure to satisfy both sweet and savoury cravings.

Ingredients:

- *4 duck breasts*
- *2 cups of white rice, boiled as instructed on packet*
- *1 chopped cucumber*
- *1 lime*
- *5 Tablespoons of chopped coriander*
- *3 tablespoons of hoisin sauce*

Instructions:

- Juice the lime into a bowl with the chopped cucumber and roughly chop coriander. Mix the cucumber, lime juice and coriander together and save until later.
- Next, prepare the duck breasts by scoring the skin gently in a criss-cross pattern.
- Season each of the duck breasts with a pinch of salt and a grind of black pepper. Put duck breast skin-side down into frying pan on medium heat. Cook for 5-7 mins until the skin is golden brown and crispy.
- Turn the duck breasts over, brown the flesh side for 2 mins and pour in 2 tbsp. of hoisin sauce. Roll the duck breasts around in the sauce and then transfer them to a baking tray.
- Put the duck breasts in the oven and roast for 7 mins if you like them medium. Cook for 5 mins if you like your duck rare or cook for 15 mins for well done.
- When the duck is cooked, take it out of the oven and pop it back into the frying pan you used earlier. Add the remaining hoisin

sauce to the pan, coat your duck breasts with the sauce and leave for 5 mins.

- As the duck cools, fluff up your rice with a fork. Slice your duck breast widthways into five or six pieces.

Spoon a generous amount of rice onto your plates, top with cucumber, coriander and lime juice and then finish with your sliced duck breast. Drizzle over your hoisin sauce and enjoy.

HEALTHY

SALMON AVOCADO

Time to Make: 35 min

Calories: 258 Kcal

Serves: 3

A delicious take on the classic Japanese sushi dish, this recipe is likely to keep you going all day with 15g of protein per serving and packed with vitamins super-greens such as avocado, cucumber and edamame beans.

Ingredients:

- *½ cup of short-grained brown rice (Boiled as instructed on the packet)*
- *1 sliced cucumber*
- *½ cup edamame beans*
- *2 tablespoons of pickled ginger*
- *½ cup of grated carrot*
- *100g of salmon, cut into small chunks*
- *A pinch of sesame seeds*
- *1 sheet nori (seaweed), cut into strips 1cm across*
- *¼ cup of vinegar*
- *2 tablespoons soy sauce*
- *1 teaspoon of wasabi*

Instructions:

- Mix the rice, cucumber, avocado, edamame, grated carrot, pickled ginger, smoked salmon and a pinch of sesame seeds.
- Mix the wasabi, vinegar, and soy sauce in a separate bowl to make the dressing.
- Add dressing to the meal just before serving and top with nori strips.

AVOCADO AND CUCUMBER NOODLES

Time to Make: 40min

Calories: 187Kcal

Serves: 2

A quirky, healthy recipe guaranteed to leave any guest entertained and reaching for seconds!

Ingredients:

- *150g of sushi grade ahi tuna, chopped into 1-inch cubes*
- *1 tablespoon chopped cilantro*
- *1 peeled and cubed avocado*
- *¼ cup of finely chopped scallions*
- *1 teaspoon vinegar*
- *A dash of soy sauce*
- *2 teaspoons of sesame oil*
- *A pinch of sesame seeds*
- *2 large cucumbers, cut with a spiralizer (Blade C)*
- *Salt and pepper*
- *1.5 tablespoons of lime juice*

Instructions:

- Make the dressing by combining the sesame seeds, sesame oil, soy sauce, vinegar and scallions. Stir to mix.
- Add the tuna to the dressing and let marinade whilst you make the rest of the dish.
- Combine avocado, cilantro and lime juice in a bowl and add a pinch of salt and pepper. Whisk until creamy.
- Dry the cucumber with a paper towel and add them to the mixing bowl until they are coated.
- Place the cucumber noodles in a bowl and top with tuna and dressing.

PICKLED VEGETABLES WITH SALMON

Time to Make: 40min

Calories: 310 Kcal

Serves: 4

This dish packs a slightly stronger punch that the others but it is guaranteed to be well-received by anyone with the pallet to handle it.

Ingredients:

- *1 cup of rice, boiled as shown on packet*
- *5 baby carrots, diced*
- *3 radishes, diced*
- *1 crushed clove of garlic*
- *3 tablespoons of rice wine vinegar*
- *1 tablespoon of sea salt*
- *150g of salmon, cubed*
- *¼ chopped cilantro*
- *1 thinly sliced avocado*
- *Sesame seeds*
- *1-2 chilli peppers, sliced*
- *A dash of soy sauce*
- *2 tablespoons water*

Instructions:

- Mix carrots, radishes, garlic, vinegar and salt in a bowl and let sit for 15min until vegetables are soft.
- Mix the chilli peppers, soy sauce, lemon juice, and water in a bowl. Add the salmon and cilantro, mix to combine.
- Spoon into serving bowls.

VEGAN TOFU POKE BOWLS

Time to Make: 25min

Calories: 450Kcal

Serves: 4

A vegan take on the Hawaiian classic. This dish is perfect for those who want the authentic Poke-Experience, but would rather skimp on the fish.

Ingredients:

- *200g of firm tofu, cut into 1-inch chunks*
- *2 tablespoons of coconut oil*
- *1 tablespoon of grated ginger*
- *1 tablespoon of low sodium tamari*
- *3 tablespoons of coconut sugar*
- *1tablespoon of sriracha sauce*
- *A pinch of salt*
- *4 cups of brown rice, boiled as instructed on the packet*
- *¼ cup of rice wine vinegar*
- *1 tablespoon of sesame oil*
- *2 tablespoons of soy sauce*
- *2 tablespoons of coconut sugar*
- *4 tablespoons of olive oil*
- *½ tablespoon of sriracha*
- *Salt and Pepper*

Instructions:

- Dry tofu on paper towels for 10 min
- Heat coconut oil over a medium heat, add tofu and fry until all sides are crispy
- Mix sesame oil, ginger, sriracha and coconut sugar. Add to tofu and fry until it is caramelised.
- To make the dressing mix vinegar, sesame oil, tamari, sugar, oil and sriracha in a bowl. Add a pinch of salt and pepper.
- Fill each bowl with rice and a drizzle of dressing, add the tofu and serve.

- For a more exciting dish, add edamame and mango to the final mix.

PALEO CARROT POKE BOWL

Time to Make: 40m

Calories: 372 Kcal

Serves: 2

A lightweight, paleo-inspired dish full of nutrients and super-greens such as carrots, sea beans and kelp.

Ingredients:

- 2 cups of rainbow carrots, cubed and steamed for 5 min
- 2 cups of Salicornia
- 2 cups of kelp noodles
- 3 tablespoons of canola oil
- A pinch of white sesame seeds
- A pinch of black sesame seeds
- 1 tablespoon of soy sauce
- 1 tablespoon of wasabi
- 1 tablespoon of sesame oil and hot chili

Instructions:

- Soak noodles in hot water for 30min, snip into 5cm lengths.
- Mix noodles, salicornia, with wasabi paste and algae oil.
- Mix carrots with sesame seeds, soy sauce, sesame oil, and hot chilli.
- Combine in a serving bowl.

MANGO HALIBUT

Time to Make: 10m
Calories: 504 Kcal
Serves: 2

A sweet and savoury Poke bowl that is the perfect warm-weather flavour, available year-round

Ingredients:

- *3 cups Spring Mix Greens- Salad*
- *2 cups raw halibut*
- *1/4 cup mango*
- *1/4 cup avocado*
- *3 Tablespoon of Shredded Coconut*
- *2 Tablespoon of soy sauce*
- *2 Tablespoon of Onions, Green, Raw*
- *2 Tablespoon of Nuts, macadamia nuts, raw*
- *2 Tablespoon of Honey*

Instructions:

- Pour soy sauce with honey on halibut and let sit for 5min
- Add mango, avocado, and coconut
- Add to a serving bowl and scoop poke mix with salad on top
- Add a pinch of macadamias with green onions on top

JICAMA AND TURMERIC POKE

Time to Make: 15min

Calories: 164 Kcal

Serves: 2

Combining the vitamin benefits of turmeric and the deliciousness of crunchy jicama, this dish is chocked full of goodness.

Ingredients:

- *3 cups kale*
- *2 cups Jicama*
- *1 cup mango*
- *1 medium Mushroom*
- *1 Tablespoon ofp Mayo*
- *1/2 Tablespoon ofp Chili Paste*
- *1/2 teaspoon of Turmeric*

Instructions:

- Add chili paste, mayonnaise, and turmeric to a bowl and mix
- Add jicama and mix until coated
- Serve with Kale and mushroom.

TUNA QUINOA WATERMELON POKE

Time to Make: 15min
Calories: 160Kcal
Serves: 3

An East Asian-inspired raw dish that masterfully pairs varying textures to deliver the perfect summer meal.

Ingredients:

- *A dash of Soy sauce*
- *1 cup of quinoa, boiled in hot water for 5 min*
- *200g of cubed watermelon (1 inch)*
- *100g of raw sushi-grade tuna, cubed*
- *1 ½ Tablespoons of sesame oil*
- *1 juiced lemon*
- *1 diced avocado*
- *3 green onions, sliced*
- *200g of sliced kale leaves*

Instructions:

- Mix quinoa with kale.
- Mix watermelon with soy sauce, sesame oil and the lemon juice in a bowl and leave in fridge until ready to serve.
- Place Quinoa and kale at base of serving bowl, add watermelon, tuna avocado and green onions. Then serve.

CHICKEN CAESAR POKE

Time to Make: 35 min

Calories: 384 Kcal

Serves: 3

The classic salad but with a Hawaiian twist, this dish brings some much-welcome familiarity to the Poke-Bowl craze.

Ingredients:

- 6 cloves of garlic, minced
- ¼ cups of mayonnaise
- 4 filleted anchovies
- 3 tablespoons of parmesan cheese, grated
- ½ teaspoon of Dijon mustard
- 1 teaspoon of lemon juice
- Salt and pepper
- ¼ cup of olive oil
- 2 cups of croutons
- 1 head of lettuce, torn into bite-size pieces
- 200g of pineapple, cubed

Instructions:

- Mix garlic, mayo, anchovies, 1 tablespoon of parmesan cheese, mustard and lemon juice. Add salt and pepper. Refrigerate for 20 min.
- Place lettuce into a Large Bowl and add dressing, pineapple, cheese and croutons. Serve cold.

MUSHROOM-TOFU POKE

Time to Make: 30 min
Calories: 300 Kcal
Serves: 4

Whilst many Poke dishes have a heavy Japanese influence, this one is especially reminiscent of the land of the rising sun.

Ingredients:

- *Brown rice, boiled as directed on packet*
- *Tofu, cut into cubes and dried*
- *2 eggs, boiled for 10 min and peeled*
- *Mangetout*
- *Edamame beans, raw or boiled until soft*
- *Celery, boiled until soft and chopped into 1-inch pieces*
- *Sweetcorn*
- *Beetroot, sliced into very thin strips*
- *Spring onions, sliced*
- *Japanese Pickles*

Instructions:

- Pan fry tofu over a medium heat until golden brown on all sides.
- Cut the eggs in half
- Mix the Mangetout, beetroot, edamame beans, celery, sweetcorn and spring onions.
- Add the Brown rice at the base of a serving bowl. Add vegetable mix on top and place boiled egg on surface.
- Divide into 4 and serve.

TUNA-AVOCADO BOATS

Time to Make: 20min
Calories: 360 Kcal
Serves: 8

A millennial combination of Californian and Hawaiian cuisine, Replacing the bowl for avocados, these quirky yet delicious boats serve as a perfect appetiser for any meal.

Ingredients:

- *100g sushi-grade tuna, diced*
- *¼ cup coconut aminos*
- *1 tablespoon sesame oil*
- *1 cucumber, diced*
- *3 tablespoons macadamia nuts, chopped*
- *1 tablespoon sesame seeds, for garnish*
- *8 avocados, halved longways*

Instructions:

- Mix tuna, cucumber, macadamia, coconut aminos and sesame oil seeds in a large bowl. Place in fridge for 10 min.
- Remove the seed from the avocado and place mix into hole.
- Add sesame seeds on top.

VEGGIE AND PESTO

Time to Make: 10min
Calories: 270 Kcal
Serves: 8

A Mediterranean-inspired dish, these bowls combine the flavours of Italy with the produce of Spain to create a delicious appetiser.

Ingredients:

- *500g of green pesto*
- *¾ cups of red cabbage, shredded*
- *¾ cups of cucumber, sliced into 1cm strips*
- *2 spring onions, sliced along width and separated*
- *2 tablespoons of lemon juice*
- *2 tablespoons of olive oil*
- *Salt and pepper*

Instructions:

- Mix cabbage, cucumber, spring onions, lemon juice, olive oil and a pinch of salt and pepper to create the veggie mix.
- Add the pesto and mix well.
- Serve in bowl within 2 hours.

Time to Make: 25 min
Calories: 359 Kcal
Serves: 6

A vegan dish that will leave you harking for the countryside, this bowl combines nutmeg, miso and soy with deliciously juicy portobello mushrooms.

Ingredients:

- *1/4 cup arame*
- *6 large portobello mushrooms, gills scraped away with spoon, cut into 1 inch chunks.*
- *2 tablespoons of sesame oil*
- *1 pinch ground nutmeg*
- *1/4 cup dry white wine*
- *4 tablespoon lemon juice, divided*
- *1 tablespoon of miso paste*
- *1 tablespoon of soy sauce*
- *1 medium tomato, diced into 1/2-inch chunks*
- *2 green onions, thinly sliced*
- *1 pinch red pepper flakes*
- *3 cups mixed salad greens (lettuce, cucumber, kale, spinach)*
- *1 tablespoon of white sesame seeds*

Instructions:

- Mix arame with ½ cup of hot water until soft.
- Heat sesame oil in a pan over a high heat, add mushrooms and nutmeg, cook for 3 minutes.
- Add wine and 2 tablespoons of lemon juice, cook for 5 minutes.
- Whisk together miso, tamari and remaining lemon juice. Mix with tomato, green onions, and red pepper flakes. Add mushrooms and arame, mix well.
- Season with salt and pepper and serve over salad greens, Then serve.

DATE AND MIXED FRUIT

Time to Make: 10 min
Calories: 180 Kcal
Serves: 2

A combination of sweet flavours give rise to this easy-going dish. Perfect for breakfast of a light appetiser.

Ingredients:

- *1 cup of brown rice, boiled as shown on the packet*
- *50g of dates*
- *1 apricot, cut into small chunks*
- *1 tangerine, peeled and separated into wedges*
- *1 mango, cut into small chunks*
- *50g of pine nuts*
- *A dash of coconut aminos*

Instructions:

- Mix the rice, dates and mango in a bowl.
- Add the tangerine on top along with the pine nuts.
- Add the coconut aminos and serve immediately.

RAINBOW POKE

Time to Make: 40min

Calories: 390 Kcal

Serves: 2

A fun and colourful recipe suitable for vegans. It goes great with a peanut-based sauce.

Ingredients:

- *Carrots, cut into matchstick-size pieces*
- *Cucumbers, cut into matchstick-size pieces*
- *Red cabbage, shredder*
- *Curry hummus*
- *White rice, boiled as instructed on the package*
- *Peanuts and cilantro*
- *Spinach*
- *Lettuce leaves, shredded*
- *¾ cup peanut butter*
- *¼ cup soy sauce*
- *¼ cup rice vinegar*
- *¼ cup water*
- *2 tablespoons honey*
- *1 clove garlic*

Instructions:

- To make the peanut sauce pass the peanut butter, the soy sauce, the rice vinegar, the water, the honey and the garlic through a blender until smooth, then place in fridge for 10 min.
- Mix all other ingredients in a bowl.
- Serve and add peanut butter dressing.

WATERMELON POKE

Time to Make: 4 hours (with marinade)

Calories: 386 Kcal

Serves: 4

Swapping marinated tuna for watermelon, this vegan poke bowl is healthy, colourfull and still manages to be a filling meal.

Ingredients:

- *2 cups watermelon, cut into 1-inch cubes*
- *3 Tablespoon of soy sauce*
- *2 Tablespoon of sesame oil*
- *1 Tablespoon of sesame seeds*
- *4 scallions, finely chopped (pale green part only)*
- *¼ teaspoon of agave nectar*
- *½ teaspoon of rice vinegar*
- *1 cup cooked brown rice*
- *1 Persian cucumber, thinly sliced*
- *1 medium carrot, shredded*
- *1 avocado, thinly sliced*

Instructions:

- Whisk together the soy sauce, sesame oil, sesame seeds, scallions, agave, and rice vinegar.
- Add watermelon to the marinade, mix until the watermelon is coated. Place cling film over the bowl and leave in the fridge for 4 hours.
- Add the rice to the bottom of the bowl and place the watermelon on it without the rest of the marinade sauce.
- Add cucumber, carrot and avocado. Serve immediately.

SUMMARY

As we have seen, the poke bowl is beautiful in its simplicity, yet it allows for a great deal of freedom, variation and expression in the way it is prepared. From Hawaiian classics, to oriental roots, to Mediterranean fusions; poke bowls embody a lot of what is sought after in today's cuisine: simplicity, adaptability, convenience and, above all, deep and amazing flavour. As the world becomes more complex and our lives are increasingly filled with new, fast changing innovations, the poke-bowl, with its simplicity and character, is expertly poised to become the next generation's food style of choice.

Made in United States
North Haven, CT
04 January 2022

14149994R00038